CLAWING YOUR WAY TO THE MIDDLE

CLAWING YOUR WAY TO THE MIDDLE

*An overdue tribute to the worth
and wonder of mediocrity*

dick jackman

This book was printed in the United States of America.

DEDICATED . . .

... to first base coaches,
proctologists and all others
whose job descriptions do not
 fully reflect their value to society.

This salute to mediocrity is
intended to capture the essence
of being ordinary.

It is not well-written. It is not
meant to be. Achieving literary
excellence to describe mediocrity
 would be self-defeating.

Be content that finally we have
the kind of book we can put down.

AUTHOR'S NOTE

At a time when our national security capability can monitor phone calls and sophisticated computer communications, the reader should find comfort in the knowledge that every word of *"Clawing Your Way To The Middle"* was written on a Royal 440 Standard typewriter.

Although no evidence exists that the code on the Royal 440 has ever been cracked, it is only prudent to report that two men in suits have been spotted, rummaging through my trash, looking for used typewriter ribbons.

Their efforts will be unproductive for they do so without knowing that is exactly how I obtained the ribbons in the first place, by ransacking other people's trash.

The typewriter ribbon, like mediocrity, has become undervalued. Both appear to be making a comeback. Just in time.

*Fame is fleeting, but you can take obscurity
with you when it's your time to go.*

SOMETHING SPECIAL CALLED MEDIOCRITY

Any reasonable analysis of reality will reveal that without mediocrity, civilization would come to a standstill.

It really gets down to simple mathematics.

Half of all the people on Planet Earth are *above average*. An equal number are *below average*.

Only a select few of us can *actually* be *average*, can claim to be "*TMs*" — the *Truly Mediocre*.

History has largely, perhaps deliberately, ignored the influence of the *Truly Mediocre*, choosing to overlook the fact that if it weren't for the underachievers, nobody would be defined as outstanding. The raw power of being ordinary is awesome.

The truth is that the "above average" depend upon the mediocre to fulfill their minimum daily requirement for superiority. Having someone else *"one down"* enables them to be *"one up."*

The contribution doesn't stop there. Those who are *"below average"* also rely on the *Truly Mediocre*. They view them as role models. Stretch goals. They encourage dreams of a day when underachievers can claw their way to the middle, when they can become as consistently incompetent as those who have already earned middle-of-the-pack status.

This flexibility of the few — to be scorned as inferiors by some and admired as heroes by others — remains the untold story of our time. Academia won't teach it. Researchers look the other way. Government is silent. A conspiracy is suspected.

Despite this curtain of quiet, mediocrity is proudly on display every day, its value clearly illustrated.

Teachers can't do without "C" students. Secretly, they treasure them, because without *so-so* classroom performers, it would be much more difficult to identify the "A" students.

Every year in America about 75,000 new attorneys emerge from the nation's law schools. Since lawyers cannot be relied upon to die or be disbarred at a parallel rate, it is important that half of them be mediocre. When they get into the courtroom, somebody has to lose.

We require a certain percentage of mediocre doctors. Otherwise, malpractice suits, a fundamental cornerstone of our economy, would evaporate. We'd all live too long. Homes for Assisted Dying would be overcrowded. Insurance companies would struggle. Funeral businesses would downsize. Florists would have to survive on senior prom corsages.

This institutional dependency on mediocrity extends, of course, to business, government, skateboarding, mud wrestling and all other organizational structures that sustain the human condition.

It is the denial of the worth of the *Truly Mediocre* that hurts. The refusal to acknowledge that mediocrity sets the standards for all human endeavors is a shame that has been passed from generation to generation.

The daily deeds of those of us who are *Truly Mediocre* are seldom recognized. There are no lifetime achievement awards for the ordinary. No Presidential Medals. The Nobel Prize Committee won't return our phone calls.

How can our dedication be so invisible?

- We are the ones who sit in the middle seats on airplanes.

- We worry about Global Cooling.

- We are the ones who buy the bad books, see the movies rated with only one star, are always *"It"* in tag.

- In the school chorus we moved our lips, but were never allowed to actually utter a sound. In the school play we were listed as "third bystander."

- In Monopoly, we do not aspire to a hotel on Boardwalk or Park Place, but are perfectly content with a rental on Marvin Gardens.

- It is us who regard "right-turn-on-red" as both a term of empowerment and a cultural breakthrough.

- We answer telemarketer calls, valuing them as confirmation of their personal interest in our well-being.

- We are the ones who actually answer the letters from *Publishers Clearinghouse* and then don't leave home for a year expecting a knock on the door at any moment.

- We never reject the wine or send back the steak.

- In the "Ten-Items-Or-Less" line we would make two trips rather than go over the limit by slipping an extra bag of Oreos into the cart.

- Our bumper sticker makes it clear that we are perfectly willing to permit the day to elapse unseized.

It is probably not surprising that no one is staying up late chipping away on Mount Rushmore in order to honor the ordinary. It has been apparent throughout my life that I and a few select others are destined to carry the staggering burden of permanent potential.

Webster's dictionary defines "mediocre" as "neither very good nor very bad." We know little, but we know it fluently. We search quietly for the proper manila envelope in which to file ourselves. We maintain a firm grasp of the obvious, our faces unclouded by thought.

Some people say that the *Truly Mediocre* have no depth. Not true. We have a lot of depth, but it's on the surface.

Still, we are a proud people. We excel at creating low expectations, and celebrate meeting them. We cling to the workplace principle that action is the last resort of those who have not yet learned how to postpone a decision.

A parade is not a parade unless there is someone there to watch it. That's what we — the *Truly Mediocre* — do, sit on the curb and cheer as the band marches and the music trumpets the skills of people who actually know what they're doing.

To correct the neglect of those left on the curb, to properly bring prestige to the forgotten few who have unwaveringly devoted their lives to fine-tuning the fundamentals of mediocrity, perhaps the first step is to return to one's foundation — to that moment of self-discovery when I first learned that my mission in life was to paint the town beige.

Lesson Learned: That the Truly Mediocre avoid discussion of controversial topics. We stay away from religion, politics, global warming. We will not be trapped into taking a firm stand on any issue. Instead, we rely on a lively exchange about the weather, recipes for omelets and personal experiences with mulch.

GETTING YOUR ANXIETY BETTER ORGANIZED

The perspective of the *Truly Mediocre* can be illustrated by this exchange between two guys standing on opposite banks of a river.

First guy says, "How do I get on the other side of the river?"

The other guy says, "You are on the other side of the river."

What's unique about being a "*TM*" is the clear definition of its characteristics.

There is no gray area. No mystery. You are truly mediocre or you're not. You are never on one side of the fence or the other. You straddle it. There are no degrees of being so-so.

Indecision may or may not be your problem.

In a store I have the kind of face that looks like it's already been waited on, so being ignored by a clerk can't faze me. I find comfort in the knowledge that I have earned my anonymity.

It would be misleading to mistake my behavior for timidity. It's much more than that. It is fundamental contentment with the blandness that is a pre-existing condition among those of us who are gifted with genuine mediocrity.

I trace the origins of my own mediocrity to my childhood, when I first discovered that I had an inferiority complex, although it was not a very good one.

I grew up on a farm in Iowa, the youngest of a half-dozen children, a sixth-round draft choice. The fact that the other five became outstanding achievers in their lifetimes serves to confirm that the *Truly Mediocre* are not born — they have to be trained.

My stubborn refusal to be swept up in a tide of sibling excellence verifies that once a person uncovers the worth and wonder of mediocrity it is borderline impossible to surrender to the temptation of self-improvement.

For me, it began on that farm in the days of the Great Depression. We were probably poor. No one ever said so, but the indicators were there. We had no electricity, no indoor plumbing. I was seven before I found out that toilet paper didn't have page numbers. My clothes were hand-me-downs. I thought "Clearance" was a brand name. We used to fight over who got to lick the broccoli pan.

The nearest town was six miles away. A small town. Very small. The principal industry was jury duty. The high school was so small that they taught Driver's Ed and Sex Ed in the same car.

For my early education I went to a one-room schoolhouse where one gallant woman taught all eight grades. She earned $40-a-month, with no dental plan.

I'm forever grateful to her. She taught me to adjust to reality. My handwriting was poor, but that was okay because it disguised my inability to spell. That awareness of how to make one's inadequacy work for you would become an integral element of solidifying my future mediocrity.

We did learn how to spell *hygiene*, but not how to practice it. Our drinking water was in a pail. All students in the school — maybe 16 if it was raining — used the same dipper at the water bucket. There was a level of gallantry blended with practicality in the ritual. Younger kids used the dipper first. Older pupils were next. Those with runny noses were last.

The campus had three structures — the schoolhouse and two outhouses, placed a discreet distance from each other. The playground in between gave me brief, but hollow, flirtation with achievement when I became hide-and-seek champion of the third grade. Later I discovered the reason. No one would come looking for me. Surely, paranoia could not be far behind.

During the fifth, sixth and seventh grades, I was the only one in my class.

After my third year as the entire student body of my class, I experienced a turning point that elevated mediocrity into a coveted goal. My oldest sister worked in the far-away city of Des Moines, which we regarded as the Paris of the Midwest.

One weekend she came home to the farm to visit. She asked me how I was doing in school. I said, "I'm the smartest one in my class."

She, being fully aware of the classroom numbers, said, "But aren't you also the dumbest one in your class?"

My oldest brother heard this and cautioned her. He said, "You shouldn't say that to him. You may give him an inferiority complex."

My sister responded, "Impossible. You can't have an inferiority complex if you truly *are* inferior."

I thought about that. A lot. Suddenly, I understood that I had something of my own. I realized that if I could master mediocrity while all others were chasing excellence, this could be the start of something ordinary. While everyone else was trying to be the best, I could take on the challenge to become very good at being unexceptional.

I had found my niche.

At about the same time something else happened to encourage me. Farming was not going well for us and my Dad was about ready to give it all up and try something else. But then in an incredible stroke of timing the federal government stepped in to announce a new program that would pay farmers for *not farming*!

Right away that captured our attention. The first phase of this program was to pay farmers for not raising hogs. We looked at that and said, "We can handle that!"

So, we assessed our capabilities and made a commitment to *not* raise 200 hogs. And we did this. And we did it well. So well, that the government sent us a check for $4000. The following year, based on our accelerated learning curve, we doubled our quota, promising to *not* raise 400 hogs.

But this never did work out. The application forms became complicated. The paperwork backed up on us. It was a clear case of trying to grow too big, too soon.

Still, there was a dividend. In the early stages of my mediocrity, I learned that I was not alone. Governmental bureaucracy was way ahead of me in not knowing what they were doing, but in being very good at it.

I was beginning to grasp what "state-of-the-art" really meant, the ability to make an orderly transition from one failure to the next, to replace an old crisis you worried about with a new one that produced even more anxiety.

Don't solve problems. Endure them. Until they go away out of sheer boredom. I was learning a new kind of leadership, that charisma is curable if detected early.

Lesson Learned: There are those who say that mediocrity was invented by government bureaucrats. That is unfair. However, they can take some measure of credit for elevating mediocrity to its current level of popularity.

Scientists study gravity to see why bread
doesn't land jelly-side up. The Truly Mediocre
solve the problem by putting jelly on both sides.

HONORING MEDIOCRITY'S PROUD HISTORY

Leaders claim that they learn from the mistakes of others. They seem unwilling, however, to recognize that some of us have to be "the others." They refuse to publicly acknowledge that it is our consistent lowering of the bar that permits them to boast about having raised it.

Leaders point to their ability to rouse followers in the pursuit of change-making actions. They bask in rallying the masses. They forget that the masses wouldn't be in that lethargic state if the *Truly Mediocre* hadn't first gone around the land stirring up apathy.

Leaders are organized. They tend to belong to things. They form clubs, business associations, professional groups, academic think tanks. The *Truly Mediocre* are not handicapped by unity. Even if we tried to organize, we would find that all the good acronyms have already been taken.

Unlike others who go drifting and dreaming through life, never experiencing the joyous numbness of mediocrity, right from the start I was in touch with my inner oblivion.

Lack of ambition. Absence of imagination. Aversion to risk. My qualifications overflowed. Mediocrity was there for me to claim.

Strangely, many back away from it. They go into denial that such a condition exists in their world. Self-help books and motivational programs have shouted the appeal of excellence so loudly that the sound has drowned out the voice of those who skillfully practice the ordinary.

The willingness, by some of us, to make an unselfish commitment to ineptness has been persistently overlooked by those who chronicle human history.

Proper respect for the role of mediocrity in our civilization can only be attained by understanding that the superstars of history earned their acclaim, their reputations for greatness, through the ages because there was always an adequate supply of non-performers available for comparisons.

9

- Did watching his father struggle as a bankrupt butcher inspire Shakespeare to say, "I think I'll get out of the retail meat business and try something else?"

- Who sanded and spackled before Michelangelo brought his paintbrush to the chapel?

- When Betsy Ross diversified into the flag business, to whom did she outsource the work?

- Hank Aaron and Babe Ruth hit all those home runs, but who were the pitchers who served up so many middle-of-the-plate mistakes to them?

- What part did the double-doubters have in motivating Robert Fulton to invent the steamboat as they sat on the banks of the Hudson River and shouted, "It'll never start," and when it did, adjusted their second-guessing to, "It'll never stop!"

- Why do we applaud the Tennessee legislator who in 1920 cast the turning-point vote assuring passage of the 19th Amendment (women's right-to-vote), but we forget the woman, his mother, who sent him a note: "Son, do the right thing."

History is in a hurry. It seldom stops to note the loyal mediocre. Oh, it will pause to pay paragraphs to colossal failures — the *Titanic*, the *Edsel*, creamed dried beef on toast — but these are the catastrophic consequences generated by bright people who had a bad day. To qualify as *Truly Mediocre*, people must prove their plainness over an extended period of time.

One of my heroes is an invisible person at my insurance company. He/she has style.

After buying a home some years ago, I took out a policy on the place. When the first monthly bill arrived, it included coverage for a garage on my property. What made this communication entertaining was the fact that the property *did not have a garage.*

That oversight on the part of the builder did not discourage my insurance company. As I paid the bill each month, I deleted the amount of the premium they had designated for the garage I did not have.

Their letters grew more militant, taking on a threatening tone. There was even legal department talk, warning me that they might drop the coverage of the garage I did not have. I admired this kind of innovation and my responses became very positive. Consistent incompetency deserves to be rewarded.

In my letters I began to suggest ways in which they could grow their business. I sent along a list of other buildings I did not own — a barn, a shed, a silo, the Empire State Building.

It was then that I recognized what was happening. This company, known for its excellence, was dabbling in the mediocre, trying to get a foothold among the inept. They were in over their head, but it was a noble attempt. They recognized what I would come to learn — that if you could combine mediocrity with power, all things were possible.

Putting power into the hands of the incompetent could lead to staggering results. But more about politics later.

What confronts us is history's benign neglect of the *Truly Mediocre*. We cheer forever the achiever. We print volumes on her/his deeds. No parallel praise is heaped upon the chronically inept, those who daily walk that high wire between being not-too-good and not-too-bad.

Although a permanent site for the proposed *Institute for the Ordinary* has not yet been selected (the first choice of having it on the second floor of a Dairy Queen proved unworkable), there are some pending plans for signage. In Velcro, of course. Easily detached.

To develop an improved national appreciation of the value of mediocrity's finest contributions, a major communications program is needed. Then the public will learn something about the "*TM*" lifestyle.

- *That* we make money the old-fashioned way, by falling down and suing people.

- *That* we envy the witness protection program because it appeals to our sense of obscurity.

- *That* we know if we make a mistake in the workplace, and keep on making it, it will become company policy.

- *That* we are capable of scheduled mood changes. We can go from arrogant ignorance to thoughtful uncertainty on almost any topic.

11

- *That* we are never lost, but we do frequently change where we say we're going.

There are those who feel mediocre people lack creativity. Not so. The *Truly Mediocre* are capable of coming up with many innovations. Their ability to surface new ideas is their strength. Not following through on those ideas is their consistency.

Some years ago I created *False Front, Inc.* This company had one clear-cut mission — to submit losing bids on government contracts. Since government was requiring multiple bids and every other firm was trying to win, the market was wide open for a company with solid credentials for coming in second.

We thought it through. There was risk. Supposing we should win? That would put us out of business since we had no capability to perform, only to submit bad bids.

I couldn't do this alone. I contacted other *Truly Mediocre* people whose ineptness I trusted. We tried to have meetings, but wouldn't tell each other where they were to be held. As a result, *False Front, Inc.* never got off the ground, but many of its founding principles continue to endure.

Historians would do well to take note that mediocrity, too, has its heroes. It's just that we don't know who they are.

Lesson Learned: *When you're drawing up your invitation list to a party, be sure to include an ample number of dull people. Every guest cannot be the life-of-the-party. You must have some who will laugh at the old jokes, praise the cheese dip, and leave early.*

The company called a meeting on absenteeism
and tardiness. Most people didn't show up,
and those who did were late.

RUNNING IN PLACE, AS AN ART FORM

Shortly after the time the comic book character "Superman, the Man of Tomorrow" was created, I came up with "Inferiorman, the Man of the Day Before Yesterday." But it never did catch on.

Mediocrity is not, and never has been, the sole possession of one particular profession. Any attempt by business or education or government to monopolize ineptness in a free society would be doomed by the competitive zeal of other institutions, unwilling to yield their own claim to incompetency.

That pride in the ordinary shows itself in varying patterns.

In industry, for example, there are levels of prestige involved in being appointed to groups assigned to *"study"* things. You can become a member of a committee. This guarantees you will end up in a conference room that has a table and chairs. People will fill those chairs and almost immediately discover that their principal responsibility is to agree on a date for the next meeting.

There is much more prestige, however, in being assigned, not to a committee, but to a *"Task Force."* The label itself carries with it a kind of militaristic charisma, suggesting urgency and significance, neither of which will be apparent in deliberations. What distinguishes a *"Task Force"* from a committee is the quality of the pastry and the thickness of the binders summarizing the group's work.

The highest form of group therapy in business is to be selected for the *"Strategic Planning Team."* The word *"team"* conveys a false sense of cooperation and coordination. It is a morale-boosting word suggested by the group's consultant who got his job because he was too smart to work for the company. The strategic plan is mainly an exercise in executive ego, providing them with a document for a PowerPoint presentation to a Board of Directors who will approve anything that has a pie chart and will get them to the airport on time.

It has been said that strategic plans have an additional value, in the event one should be hiking in the wilderness and run out of toilet paper.

Academia has a different approach to spinning its wheels, but is just as capable at delivering a highly sophisticated level of intellectual blandness. Educators earn a baffling degree of respect for their adeptness at securing financial grants to study problems that do not exist.

When you don't know what you're doing, simply call it basic research. This allows you the necessary license to provide a thorough analysis of the obvious. Be generous in your use of references and spray paint a few pithy quotes from out-of-town people with lengthy titles. Whatever point you are trying to make, it will sound much more authentic if it's backed up by some wisdom from Winston Churchill. *Putting the quote in italics really adds punch.*

The academic touch, envied by those who aspire to be *Truly Mediocre*, is awash in integrity. They pledge to "*study*" a problem, and that is what they do. They will not solve it, partially because there was no problem to begin with.

> (***Editing note***: The previous sentence ends with a preposition, a grammatical no-no, but totally understandable in a book about mediocrity. Here, we rely on a quote: "*Ending a sentence in a preposition is a situation up with which I will not put.*"
> Probably spoken by Winston Churchill.)

One other point on a scholar's approach to writing a paper and the refusal to bring it to a decisive conclusion. Solving a problem being "*studied*" would be counter to accepted research traditions, greatly diminishing the odds for follow-on funding to study the impact of the original indecision.

Solving the problem also risks earning the derision of academic colleagues who understand that the goal, in all disciplines, is to grow the problem until it can be turned into a course with full accreditation. This is a challenge willingly embraced by any academic worth his/her weight in websites.

Perhaps the most skilled at "*running in place*" are the politicians. Politics, being the only profession where you can get a reputation for honesty by admitting you lied, elevates inaction to Alpian heights. Their technique is to create a problem that was not previously there and then call a press conference to announce they have solved it.

Admittedly, an elected official has an edge. A congressman, for example, can hold hearings on almost any subject and disguise this activity as actual achievement. If that step is not intense enough, the next action is to go on a fact-finding tour somewhere in the world to a country with a nice beach.

A politician, with a strong skill set in inertia, can talk for two hours on any issue — four hours if he happens to know something about it. His main message is: "*Somebody ought to do something!*"

That line is from every western movie ever made. Early in the film, the townspeople, harassed by rowdy, lawless villains, meet in the church in order to list their grievances. At the peak of their desperation, someone inevitably shouts: "*Somebody ought to do something!*"

In the movie, it's only a matter of minutes before John Wayne rides into town, and in 90 minutes order is restored and the schoolmarm can sleep peacefully, and not alone. In politics that is an unacceptable outcome. Turmoil must be maintained, at least until November.

People in business, education and government understand a fundamental truth: you can't take your mediocrity for granted — you have to work at it.

And when it flourishes it can be a thing of beauty.

When I was in the Army I needed a pen to do my work. To get a pen you had to fill out a requisition form. In order to fill out the form you had to have a pen. And if you had a pen to fill out the form then you didn't need to requisition a new one.

When I was in high school our football team lost nearly every game. The one game we won was the opener. We simply weren't ready. The other team was more mediocre than we were. They had practiced harder. We won, 6-0. We missed the extra point because we had a false confidence that we would never score and therefore did not need to be prepared for the point-after-touchdown.

For the next eight games we escalated our mediocrity. We lost them all. We corrected whatever had gone wrong in that first game, the only blemish that prevented us from achieving oblivion. We were so bad our homecoming was scheduled as an away game.

The season, however, provided a window to the wonders of mediocrity. We became very popular with other teams. They would send a bus and a police escort to make sure we got to their field for the game. Schools that didn't even have football teams began to call us, trying to get on our schedule.

For me, it was a preview of coming attractions. It strengthened my hope that maybe somewhere out there in the future, I, too, could serve on a task force, or write an academic paper, or learn the basic rule of politics, that to err is human, but to blame it on somebody else — that is as good as it gets.

Lesson Learned: *I tried golf. Hit a ball into the trees. Then the water. Then the sand. Finally got on the green and had a downhill 20-footer to save my 9. I asked the caddy, "What should I do with this putt?" He said, "Try to keep it low."*

MEDIOCRE SPEAKERS DO NOT SUFFER BUTTERFLIES

There is an illusion among those who have never experienced true mediocrity that being average is easy.

Wrong.

Not just anybody can be inept at everything. Only a select few are capable of mastering such versatility. Nowhere is that skill more dramatically evident than in the field of communications. The ability to state the obvious in terms of the incomprehensible is an enviable trait.

People in high places whose excellence disqualifies them from consideration as serious contenders for mediocrity status can on rare occasions achieve a memorable level of bafflement in their messages. It's almost as if for one joyous moment they found themselves free of high expectations and went on a spree, recklessly conjugating verbs, fracturing compound sentences and splitting infinitives so that they stayed split.

In 1973 Justice William Brennan of the U.S. Supreme Court tackled the quadruple negative, a grammatical feat comparable to a trapeze performer completing a triple loop. Justice Brennan wrote:

> *"This is not to say, however, that the prima facie case may not be met by evidence supporting a finding that a lesser degree of segregated schooling in the core city area would not have resulted even if the Board had not acted as it did."*

That's right up there with: *"What is to be always could."*

The field of communications allows those who can't make the cut as an all-around mediocre individual to specialize. If you're really sincere about becoming ordinary, it's important to recognize your limitations and to cultivate them.

With specialization a realistic option, there is an unyielding urge to become really good at being average in a particular field. The sign on the door may say: *"M.D.,"* but once inside you may find he/she restricts the practice only to Ear Wax Removal or Deer Tick Bites. If clearing your nasal passages is your problem, you may have to take your co-pay down the hall.

The window of opportunity to become mediocre in a special discipline is often brief. You can't wait forever to make your choice. When the moment arrives you have to be ready.

My moment came when I realized I might be able to become a public speaker who could fill a much-needed role. The public speaking marketplace was flooded with really talented performers, each of them gifted with brilliant voices, outstanding material, spellbinding delivery.

What was missing was a stockpile of run-of-the-mill speakers.

I said to myself, *"Go for it!"*

With so many speakers compelling in their message and articulate in their command of an audience, my goal was to bring some balance to all that quality.

I became a de-motivational speaker. The timing was right. Just when America was in danger of becoming overly motivated, I faced up to the challenge of restoring a healthy blend of boredom to audiences that were becoming excessively hyped.

After-dinner speeches were my specialty. These were gatherings of people who had seen chicken prepared in every way possible; who attended in hope that they would be introduced by the emcee; who spent the evening sitting on the edge of their car keys eager to get home to their loved ones — some to their husbands and wives.

The key to my popularity as a so-so speaker was knowing that members of this audience, after a long day of work, would be overjoyed to hear from someone more incompetent than they were.

I created a brochure to advertise my strengths. I entitled it: *"America's Most Mediocre Speaker."* The text pointed out the advantages of booking a mediocre platform performer.

- A truly mediocre speaker makes all the other speakers on the program seem better than they actually are. I promised that if people thought being thoroughly bored was character-building, I was their man.

- A truly mediocre speaker is always available, easily booked on short notice, because no one else wants him. People would ask me to "*check my calendar.*" I didn't have to. I knew the date was open.

- A truly mediocre speaker doesn't cost much. I was surprised when they paid me at all. And expenses were not a big budget item. I was content to fly tourist, take the shuttle in from the airport and stay overnight in the kind of hotel where you call the desk for a towel and they tell you someone else is using it.

- A truly mediocre speaker doesn't complicate the logistics of the session by using state-of-the-art visual aids. He has a deeply rooted fear of anything high tech, and does not want the room lights lowered, for fear the audience will exit in substantial numbers.

- A truly mediocre speaker means that those in the audience won't have to take any notes. He's not going to say anything important, not going to permit substance to interfere with his remarks. This frees up the crowd to go on a mental holiday, to think of all the things they could be doing if they weren't trapped in this room.

- A truly mediocre speaker will not try to motivate you to run through a wall, scale the Alps or pass the guy ahead of you in the car wash. He doesn't want to leave you with words that will inspire you for a lifetime, just a message you will remember for as long as it takes you to get to the parking lot.

Mediocre speakers are also popular because their presentations do not lead to one of those painful "*Q and A*" sessions after the talk. Having raised no specific issues and having been delightfully vague while doing it, only one question is appropriate: "*When do we adjourn?*"

Such speakers are never nervous. They don't have butterflies. Their secret is that they overcame their fear of public speaking because of their confidence that no one would ask them to speak.

The hinges of history are oiled by spectacular orators, but it takes mediocre speakers, polished in their dullness, to sharpen the public focus on the great ones. In some ways, it's a form of public service.

Lesson Learned: Butterflies are delightfully independent. They are not organized, seldom fly in formation. Unlike birds. Birds have staff meetings. That's where they make their plans to peel off in flight and strafe-bomb your newly-washed car.

The Truly Mediocre do not fear heights.
We fear widths.

THE THRILL OF LUKEWARM

Curiosity about the subject of mediocrity in recent years has intensified to a frenzied level of lethargy, the highest standard of popularity achievable under standards set by the *Institute for the Unspectacular*, mediocrity's governing board of oversight.

This renewed public interest can be measured in the volume of mail that has soared from a drip to a trickle.

In that mail are questions. Not on burning issues. If you live in the world of the *Truly Mediocre*, there are no burning issues. Only smoldering embers.

The inquiries are often borderline excellent, with the power to elevate our paranoia to new heights of suspicion. The people who submit such penetrating questions do not fool us. We are onto them. We recognize them as intellectual missionaries trying to bait us into providing intelligent answers.

That won't happen. The *Truly Mediocre* have been too ordinary for too long to be intimidated by that ploy which seeks only to trick us into abandoning our commitment to be unexceptional. We value the vague, and the sample correspondence printed here will reflect the integrity of that dedication.

Q. Is mediocrity a gift of birth or can it be acquired through life experience?

A. Most *Truly Mediocre* people are self-made. There is insufficient data available to suggest that heredity can be relied upon to achieve middle-of-the-pack status. Too often, some member of the family will run off and become really accomplished. They are seduced by ambition. Then optimism sets in and they forget the basic philosophy of the mediocre — that the glass is neither half empty nor half full. It is dirty and it's our job to clean it.

Q. Does the mediocrity movement have a leader?

A. No. That would be counter-productive.

Q. Can you be mediocre and *not* know it?

A. Not likely. The *Truly Mediocre* believe that anything to be perfectly spontaneous must be carefully rehearsed. Our mood swings are scheduled. We don't get face lifts — we have our bodies lowered. Knowing who you are *not* is mediocrity's finest hour.

Q. Does charisma eliminate one's chances of joining the ranks of the *Truly Mediocre?*

A. Automatically. That's why you won't find any airline pilots, gym teachers or chain-smoking cafeteria workers at our meetings. Even accountants who have had their charisma surgically removed are barred. It may grow back. People with power to flaunt are ineligible. Flagmen on highway construction projects. People who look under the hoods of cars. Anyone with a clipboard. Such individuals lack the understanding that every day has its decisions, and if you can avoid them, you have a chance of becoming *Truly Mediocre.*

Q. If I'm serious about seeking mediocrity, are there places where I can go to learn?

A. Most any staff meeting will do. Observe closely. A staff meeting is held because there was one last week. It's a good place in which to avoid eye contact, practice weak handshakes, make excuses, blame others and update your meteorological expertise (*"Do you think it will rain?"*).

While universities will not openly acknowledge instruction in mediocrity in their course catalogs because it has a negative impact on parental willingness to cough up tuition money for kids they're trying to get out of the house, if you can establish friendships with proven "C" students you can pretty well nail down the course load that will escort you unnoticed to a diploma without cluttering up your mind with knowledge. (That sentence has 70 words — a reach for the *Truly Mediocre*, but an example of our rare risk-taking.)

Q Is it useful to learn how to procrastinate?

A. Quite useful, but it's something you can put off for awhile.

Q. What goes through the minds of the *Truly Mediocre*?

A. A "*TM*" is a realist. We know that good news never comes in brown envelopes. That a filing cabinet enables you to lose things systematically. That if you want to find your scissors, look for your stapler, which will be empty, as all staplers are meant to be. That if your boss delivers a message that is particularly clear, chances are you misunderstood him/her. That things worth worrying about include:

(a) How does anyone get off a non-stop flight?

(b) Whatever happened to *Preparation A through G* and who got that research funded?

(c) Why do croutons come in air-tight packages?

(d) In real life, the hare wins the race and *Goliath* is still a 30-point favorite over *David* in the re-match.

Q. Is there recommended reading for the mediocre mind set?

A. Entire forests have been cut down to supply the paper on which you can find the stuff guaranteed to numb your mind — minutes from your nearest PTA meeting; the complete body of work of any state legislature; anything written attempting to explain what Picasso really meant; directions on how to assemble whatever it was Santa Claus left behind, without batteries.

For the convenience of those with a genuine interest in discovering and treasuring their own inadequacy, a *Top Ten* list of self-help literature has been compiled:

1. "Creative Suffering, Self-taught"

2. "A Beginner's Guide to Self-Pity"

3. "All Chocolate Bunnies are Hollow"

4. "Overcoming Peace of Mind"

5. "Amnesia Déjà vu — Forgetting Again What You Forgot Before."

That's the Top Ten list. It should be noted that in the world of mediocrity, all lists are partial.

All of this literature has been reviewed by critics. The reviews were so-so. Perfect.

Lesson Learned: *Worrying is a skill you can develop. Back in the days of pay toilets, I worried about whether it would undermine the economy if I left the door open for the next guy.*

When giving instructions, take care to make them verbal and vague. This improves your chances of deniability in the event that whatever it is that hits the fan is not evenly distributed.

MAINTAINING ONE'S MEDIOCRITY

Mediocrity, once achieved, can, if neglected, evolve into excellence and once gone, it is difficult to reclaim.

Remaining mediocre throughout one's lifetime requires a persistent vigilance. You have to work at it.

To be genuinely ordinary over the long haul, you have to bring your "C" game every day. Part of it is developing a style.

I walk down the street. A beautiful woman approaches. She goes right by, never breaking stride. No eye contact. No nodding of her head. No winsome smile. To all outside appearances, she is ignoring me. But a *Truly Mediocre* man knows she's pretending. Behind that cool, contented exterior, surely she must be eating her heart out. She walks away. I never see her again. Happens to me a lot.

Part of what makes mediocrity so valuable is the consistent gullibility of those who practice it faithfully. The *Truly Mediocre* actually believe the stuff they hear, like:

> "Just give me your number and the doctor will call you right back."

> "Send your résumé and we'll keep it on file, and let you know when something opens up."

> "Your table will be ready in a few minutes."

> "Your luggage isn't lost, it's only misplaced."

To maintain the integrity of your commitment to mediocrity, you must study those who do it well. You can find it sometimes where you least expect it. Even the most noble of professions — medicine — has its moments.

Visit a doctor to have a sliver removed from your finger, and you may emerge with a diagnosis of Irritable Bowel Syndrome and several major diseases that are difficult to pronounce. This is called marketing.

To appreciate the power of mere words, listen to the language of medicine. Pivotal lessons can be learned in conversations with a medic that have nothing to do with anatomy.

When you have reached a peak of frenzy about why something hurts where it does, and the physician has examined you thoroughly, the moment of suspense arrives when his/her diagnosis is about to be revealed. Prepare yourself for a three-word description of your condition, three words learned the first day in medical school and never to be forgotten:

"It's not unusual."

That splendid recitation can put even the most anxious patients at ease. It's reassurance that even if the doctor hasn't the remotest idea of what your ailment is, there is instant comfort in knowing other people without a clue have the same thing.

You can't wait to make your co-pay and get to your car. You will tell your family, the neighbors, your co-workers, passing strangers and the *Associated Press* that what you have is "not unusual."

Nurses are given a different phrase to learn in their training.

Check into a hospital. At the summit of your anxiety, your attending nurse, without warning, will smile and recite the four precious words she learned on Day One in Patient Care:

"I'll be right back."

She will *not* be right back. When she leaves your room, she will exit the building, make a career change, move to another area code and leave no forwarding address.

Once you understand that the gift of permanent mediocrity has been bestowed upon you, the sensitivity to what's being said around you will improve. You understand you can learn your craft from others.

I walked into the lobby of a large government building in Washington. I said to the receptionist, *"This is a big place. How many people work here?"* She said, *"About half of them."*

The first time I drove a car into New York City I pulled up in front of a hotel. I asked the policeman standing there, *"May I park here?"* He said, *"No."* I said, *"How about all these other cars?"* He said, *"They didn't ask."*

A key skill for the mediocre who are serious about maintaining that distinction is the stockpiling of excuses for non-performance. This is particularly valuable in the workplace. Under pressure to explain why a job wasn't done, a deadline wasn't met, or why only three of the dozen doughnuts are glazed, the resourceful mid-achiever will have at his command an assortment of dependable excuses, all tested and proven by the *Truly Mediocre Standards Board*.

These are not new. They are not creative. They are not expected to be. But they are reliable no matter what the setting — business, academic, governmental — they work, if delivered with a straight face and a reasonable amount of simulated sincerity.

1. *"That's not my department."*

    Instantly absolves you of any responsibility and can be punctuated by excusing yourself to go to the restroom long enough for the subject to be dismissed before you return.

2. *"I thought we had another week on that."*

    This carries with it the subtle hint that you were misinformed by somebody. This casts a wide net of suspicion and shifts the focus from your inability to perform to the second-rate job of communications done by someone who does not exist. In the *Manual on Mediocrity*, this is referred to as *"the blame switch."*

3. *"We've never tried that before."*

    Perfect for striking terror into the bureaucratic hearts of all those who favor their pension over their passion. If necessary, you can recite a litany of things that *"might go wrong"* if this idea is pushed. Then, recommend *"tabling"* the idea until the next meeting. That will kill the project and protect you from any potential responsibility.

4. *"We've tried that before."*

This is the reverse of No. 3, and just as effective because it contains the threat of that dreaded management disease — *"failure-by-repetition."* Use selectively and deliver only after a seemingly thoughtful pause.

5. *"Let's appoint a sub-committee."*

Right up there with *"It's not in the budget,"* as a method of discouraging an idea that might trap you into responsibility for an outcome. *Note:* Try to appoint only people who are not in the room to the sub-committee. They will never be heard from again.

6. *"The Legal Department will never buy it."*

To be used only when all other excuses fail. This is sure-fire. You can send any issue to the lawyers and be assured it will disappear gracefully. Ask a lawyer, *"What time is it?"* He will say, *"How soon do you need to know?"* If you value mediocrity, these are your allies.

When in doubt, use phrases like: *"But not in the South, I don't believe."* Or: *"You can't teach an old dog new tricks."* This will brand you as a keeper of trite phrases capable of casting a pall over the room and bringing a meeting to a halt. Not a *screeching* halt. Among the mediocre, halts are whimpering, not screeching.

Lesson Learned: *The Truly Mediocre practice abstinence, but always in moderation.*

A Truly Mediocre person seldom believes what he himself says. That makes it more understandable that he can hardly control his surprise when other people actually pay attention to him.

TAKING PRIDE IN OUR GROSS NATIONAL GUILT

Part of the reward of being *Truly Mediocre* is the natural immunity one has from guilt. We have no need to distribute guilt to others, because we already know we're at fault.

We have come to terms with reality. We do not suffer the agony of suspicion that others are talking about us, because we have already convinced ourselves they are. We expect to use the salad fork on the entrée and would be lost without the subtle looks of superiority from around the table.

Comforted by our constant victimhood, we are at peace.

Those of us who have dedicated ourselves to scaling the heights of mediocrity understand the value of becoming fluent in the language of apology, uncertainty and caution.

Asked, *"How are you?"* we will reply, *"I feel more like I do now than I did before."*

Asked, *"How do you spell Mississippi?"* we will respond, *"Do you mean the river or the state?"*

Asked to write a letter of recommendation for a former employee, we will boldly state, *"When he has been with you as long as he's been with us, you'll feel about him as we do."*

We never suggest that people stop worrying. Some people enjoy worrying. They must or they wouldn't do so much of it. They should worry more, double their pleasure.

I once knew someone who worried about whether it was going to rain a week from Saturday on an event he had scheduled. I was thrilled for him. He had ten days of guaranteed anxiety ahead of him. I know people who can worry for 30 minutes on "partly cloudy." I have a policy about rain. When it rains, *I LET IT!* I have never invested any time in worrying about weather, which gives me leftover time to invest in something constructive, like apathy.

What makes the *Truly Mediocre* so special is that they are not caught up in commitment, a virtue that has been sweeping the country since the introduction of the *Peace Corps* and the decision by Public Broadcasting to teach us more than we wanted to know about the Red-Bellied Turtle. The Spotted Owl gets a lot of press. Only the mediocre will speak out for the Unspotted Owl.

While avoiding the popular wave of commitment, the mediocre remain equally untouched by the national pastime of *Guilt Distribution*, that finger-pointing recreation that has so captured mainstream America. Guilt is a growth industry. Jewish kids brag that they are born with it. Catholic kids have to go to school to fine-tune it. The rich have it, but have learned to live with it. Without guilt, greeting card sales would plummet. Telemarketers would be speechless.

Guilt Distribution has many talented practitioners. Some are born with the gift — women, life insurance salespeople, and anyone who isn't overweight.

Some deliberately set out to develop the skill. They enroll in special training courses on how to cloud the conscience of those they encounter in life. The best of these graduate to become members of the clergy or door-to-door sellers of Girl Scout cookies.

Until this paragraph, the topic of *"Women and Mediocrity"* has been avoided through the art of evasion, an essential property of the *Truly Mediocre*.

The truth is that women are rarely mediocre. They are too good at what they do. It all started with: *"In the beginning, God created man, and then took another look and said, 'I can do better than that.'"*

Oh, there are exceptions. Some women are very ordinary cooks. The only reason they have a kitchen is that it came with the house. The fact that you can't distinguish their apple pie from their meatloaf is only further evidence that women have been victimized by typecasting throughout history. Most women who can't cook are smart enough to go through life eating out, and if you're that smart, you don't qualify as *Truly Mediocre*.

A frequent target of guilt distribution is that portion of the population considered to be carrying excess poundage — guys who define a balanced meal as a hoagie in each hand; who view a toga as designer jeans; who when they get on an elevator, it better be going down; who take it as a personal insult when airlines advertise *"We fly wide bodies from coast-to-coast."*

The *Truly Mediocre* who happen to have a weight problem are unruffled by ridicule. They prefer to believe they have cultivated a natural immunity to thinness.

Perhaps the most consistent demonstration of guilt distribution can be found in something affectionately termed as *"Road Rage."* It has been with us since the invention of the automobile. It is likely that the human resentment and competitive spirit involved with transportation was present in the Horse and Buggy Era, but reports of drivers flailing each other with whips are at best fragmented.

"Road Rage" has gained peak popularity with the emergence of high speed vehicles, demolition derby expressways and a cultural acceptance of four-letter words as a means of proper social expression.

The condition is spurred by the universal belief that the automobile bestows upon its driver special powers that are not possessed by the imposters in other vehicles who are daring to share the same cement with him.

Magically, superiority sets in at the turn of the ignition. Immediately, the same guy who couldn't avoid plowing through the flower bed with his power mower is transformed into the pace car driver at the Indianapolis 500.

With that feeling comes a parallel conviction that he is exempt from the legisled speed limit. The mind set shifts. He senses a hostile environment. Those other drivers are lunatics, sent out there to impede his progress. Those traffic police are highly prejudicial tyrants who should be forbidden to mate and reproduce.

It doesn't help that the car ahead has a bumper sticker: *"My horn is broken, watch for my finger."*

Big city drivers are more adept at *Road Rage* than rural drivers. It's simply because they have more experience in being trapped in temper-to-temper traffic jams where the only way to move forward is to buy the car ahead of you.

The beauty of the *Truly Mediocre* is that we don't suffer *"Road Rage."* We cause it. We drive the speed limit. We're too placid. We're vanilla. We buy cars without horns. We think that other driver is just showing us a friendly wave of his hand and forgot to use all his fingers.

Society's Anger Index, a statistical sub-division of our Gross National Guilt, depends upon a balance between those who are outraged and those whom they are outraged at; between those who hurt other people's feelings and those who wake up each day wondering who is going to hurt their feelings that day.

Guilt, like crabgrass, can be found most anywhere. It is hereditary. Parents get it from their kids.

Real professionals — those who know how to distribute guilt while converting solvable problems into mega catastrophes — know how to make a crisis last. When they see light at the end of a tunnel, they add more tunnel.

The *Truly Mediocre* have an edge in all this turmoil. We know that our assignment is not to grow a crisis, but to ignore it; not to distribute guilt, but to absorb it. We have learned style, that what's important in life is not how to be humble when you're a success, but how to be arrogant when you're a flop.

Lesson Learned: We took a survey of a cafeteria. Two complaints dominated the results. The first complaint was the food was bad. The second complaint was the portions were too small. What that means is that people thought the food was awful — and they wanted more of it!

How do you become Truly Mediocre? Like any other
coveted prize, first there's the interview, then the
talent, swimsuit and evening gown competition.

UNDERSTANDING YOU ARE NOT ALONE

The *Truly Mediocre* have standards. We measure ourselves by the number of conflicting views we can hold on the same topic. Complacency keeps us entertained. We are capable of rationalizing almost any condition.

Earlier we mentioned the pressure overweight people are under from so many sources. But if you are fortunate to be *Truly Mediocre* at the same time you are obese, you will have trained yourself to see the positive side of those surplus calories.

Losing weight is, after careful analysis, borderline unpatriotic. Thin people contribute very little to the economy. Thin people don't eat much, and our nation's food supply is in overabundance. Thin people don't use much material in their clothing, and we know the state of our textile industry. In the shower, fat people use more soap than thin people. Fat people don't buy foreign cars.

For those of us who master the art of the ordinary, there is no anxiety about reaching one's full potential. We find comfort in knowing we have already peaked.

We do not worry about the things that trouble other minds. A mediocre man is skilled at rejection. We do not take offense at being turned down. It is a fundamental part of enriching our blandness.

It's almost another act of public service. There are women who sometimes feel a need to reject a man, just to stay in practice. That's where the *Truly Mediocre* step up. We can handle it, because we know that we cannot possibly be rebuffed unless we have first been buffed. We cannot be rejected unless first we have been jected.

Our defenses are so ingrained that insults will not disturb those of us who have accepted our mediocrity. That comfort gives us an edge over those who are not yet willing to recognize that the safe haven of mediocrityland is out of their reach. They are doomed to inhabit the turbulent world of success.

Part of what makes mediocrity so attractive to so many is that you can find it most anywhere. Anywhere, that is, except in Small Business.

Small Business people encounter small problems, and so, they solve them. They solve them because they do not have the time, personnel, financial resources and proven know-how to take a small problem and snowball it into a monumental crisis.

Big Business has no such handicap.

They have the luxury of appointing a committee. Really sophisticated companies whose executives have attended a two-week retreat and have earned a certificate in Crisis Enrichment may opt to bypass the option of naming it a committee, and instead title it as a *"task force"* or the ever-popular *"action team."*

Regardless of nomenclature, the assigned task doesn't change. The job of the study group is to thoroughly examine the problem. They can be counted on to do this. They will check to see if others faced a similar problem — vendors, competitors, the Pilgrims, the Green Bay Packers.

Weeks go by. They become months. And then one day the desired conclusion arrives. It all goes away — the problem, not the committee. That group continues to meet because the members have become socially dependent on each other and Human Resources fears a breakdown in employee morale if their sessions should cease.

Significantly, there is nothing in the company manual explaining how to dissolve committees, only how to create them. The manual itself, of course, was developed by a committee which had the foresight to build in permanence to its own existence.

Big Business mediocrity is at its best when the inactions of several departments are blended to produce a colossal outcome.

In front of Company A is a river. There is a bridge over the river with a capacity of five tons.

On Thursday morning a truck weighing ten tons tries to cross the bridge, but breaks through and plunges into the water.

That creates an instant problem at Company A. That's when the carefully constructed response plan kicks in. A committee is appointed to deal with the problem.

The committee decides the best way to solve the problem is to rent a crane, pull the truck out, repair the bridge. And so, that is done. They rent a crane, pull the truck out, repair the bridge.

And everything is fine.

Until next Thursday morning, when that same truck tries to cross the bridge, breaks through and goes into the water. Once again we have a problem at Company A. Fortunately, this time the problem is not so serious. For now we have that priceless thing in business, called "experience."

We know that last week we fixed the problem by renting a crane, pulling the truck out and repairing the bridge. Based on this accelerated learning curve, we decide to do that again.

Every Thursday morning for nine straight Thursday mornings, that truck keeps coming across the bridge, breaking through and going into the water.

In the tenth week a new consideration enters the picture — the Accounting Department. The people in Finance. They join the decision-making process because they've been getting all those bills for crane rental and they figure: *"If we need a crane this badly, we better buy one!"*

At work here are the laws of unintended consequences. It's important in these cases never to attribute to evil intention that which can be adequately explained by incompetent performance.

Business procedures are not being picked on here. Similar acts of crisis enrichment can be found in government, academia and the arts. Each will discover in their own way that a decision is something that happens when you can't get anyone to serve on a committee.

The *Official Guide to Mediocrity*, which was never quite completed, lists several helpful rules of conduct for those trying to get the hang of being ordinary.

- There is no expiration date for blaming others.

- There is nothing wrong with an idea that extended discussion won't aggravate.

- In choosing up sides in an argument remember the boss does not have a license to kill, but he does have a learner's permit.

- Avoid getting involved in anything that has to do with a *"mission statement."* You will not live long enough to see it finished.

And, of course, there is the overriding rule that governs the behavior of all who are skilled in mediocrity: *"Never get into a fight with ugly people —they have nothing to lose."*

In any conference room skirmish, the *Truly Mediocre* will not fight. They will reach for another doughnut. And look at their watch.

Lesson Learned: The Truly Mediocre — when our ship comes in, you'll find us at the airport.

In the high tech world ahead, the Truly Mediocre are betting that natural stupidity will win out over artificial intelligence.

THE FUTURE OF MEDIOCRITY

This collection of essays was intended to be a manual on how to be decisive.

But I changed my mind.

It does, however, surface a question that the *Truly Mediocre* can mull for months: *"If a book about failure doesn't sell, is it a success?"*

There are those who forecast a bleak future for mediocrity. With the flood of high technology innovations engulfing civilization, there is speculation that soon only excellence will be available to all.

To be properly dressed for the day, every person will leave home with their palm computer, wireless modem, electronic pager and a cell phone that will start your car, order your coffee, and provide advance information on which stall in the restroom has just been resupplied with toilet paper.

Can mediocrity persevere in that hostile environment?

A positive answer can be found in one's confidence that the *Truly Mediocre* can continue to spin their wheels by never giving up their basic beliefs:

- The belief that in any situation, it is within our capability to do quite efficiently that which needs not be done at all.

- The belief that we can maintain our distance from problems, knowing that one's idealism increases in direct proportion to that distance.

- The belief that no matter how many research grants are approved, science will never come up with answers to major questions, like: *"When they ship Styrofoam, what do they pack it in?"* or *"How can you tell you're running out of invisible ink?"* Scientists bypass those questions, dismissing them as trivial. Mediocre people are not so quick to ignore the quest for answers.

- The belief that creativity is overrated. When we have a letter to write, it is best to rely on the time-tested bureaucratic practice of running to the files to see what we wrote last year, fully understanding that last year we ran to the files to see what we wrote the year before. After 50 years of this, you begin calling it a "tradition."

- The belief that sleep is your most reliable ally, remembering that if you sleep eight hours a night, and live to be 75, you will have spent a quarter of a century unconscious. Not counting staff meetings.

- The belief that with a more mobile world population, mediocrity missionaries will be on the move. We'll send ours out. They'll send theirs in. This should assure the global preservation of dullness. Think China. A nation of one billion people. Even if you're one-in-a-million, there are a thousand more like you.

- The belief that more people will come to their senses and understand the value of simplicity. That their last words spoken will not be a regret that they wish they had spent more time with their computer, but that they recognize from the sign in the bank window why life is not to be taken too seriously. That sign tells you that your funds are protected by the Federal Deposit Insurance Corporation, an agency of a government trillions of dollars in debt.

There is good reason for optimism about the long-range future of mediocrity. Static cling and ring-around-the-collar may disappear, but human insecurity seems destined for a stable continuity.

Age is not a legitimate threat. One can maintain one's numbness well into the senior years. I can lend personal testimony to that. I am very good at being old. I have been old for a long time. The symptoms are all there — my knees buckle easier than my belt; when I bend over to tie my shoes, now I look around to see if there's anything else I should be doing while I'm down there; when I work out at the gym, the purpose is so I can hear heavy breathing again.

The years may advance, but my mediocrity, carefully honed for decades, remains intact. That consistency gets its substance from a lifelong experience with an unfulfilled yearning. All my life I have wanted people to ask me one question — one specific inquiry — and no one ever does.

That question is: *"Do you know how to milk a cow?"*

Because I do. I know how to milk a cow, and have ever since I was nine years old. And do you know what that teaches you? It teaches discipline, loyalty, duty. It doesn't matter where you are socially on a Sunday afternoon at 5:30 p.m. It's time to get out to that barn. It doesn't matter if the temperature is five degrees below zero the next morning at 5:30 a.m. It's time to return to that barn.

Milking cows trains you in adjusting to reality. My résumé listed this skill as a career highlight. No one paid attention to it. I went through dozens of job interviews. No one asked me: *"Do you know how to milk a cow?"*

Pretty soon I began to notice that people weren't asking me about other things I knew.

I know why the English drive on the left side of the road.

I know what time it is in Hong Kong.

I can recite the Infield Fly Rule.

No one cared.

With no public curiosity about the one thing I could do well, my cow barn capability, it is not surprising I carved out a career in mediocrity. It was the next logical place to hide.

That early recognition of the power of being ordinary — the power to make achievers feel superior and to give underachievers confidence that they could someday rise to mediocrity — it became more than a lifestyle. It was a calling.

There is a thrill in that first discovery that some people have more money than you do.

There is surprise in finding out that some people are smarter than you.

There is stunning awe in learning that some people are actually better looking than you.

But to the *Truly Mediocre*, that's okay. We have one clear-cut advantage. It doesn't really matter that others are richer, smarter, better looking, because our edge is that *no one can outwork us*. That is a decision we make for ourselves.

We, the *Truly Mediocre*, find quiet comfort in that, just as we continue to be delightfully haunted by the question that perpetually inspires us:

"If you try to fail, and you succeed, which have you done?"

Lesson Learned: *As unprepared as we are for good news, those of us who claim to be truly mediocre must face up to the possibility that things may turn out very well.*

ABOUT THE AUTHOR

Dick Jackman was born on a farm in Iowa.

He went to a one-room schoolhouse
where his career peaked when he became
Hide-and-Seek champion of the third grade.

Nothing much happened after that.

Made in the USA
Middletown, DE
24 November 2014